In the Embrace of 1959:
A Journey Through Time

Celebrating your year
1959
A memorable year for

TABLE OF CONTENTS

INTRODUCTION

TABLE OF CONTENTS

TECHNOLOGY AND INNOVATION

6

THE COST OF THINGS

7

BIRTHS IN 1959

8

Introduction

"Echoes of 1959: A Melodic Chronicle of a Transformative Era"

Embark on a nostalgic voyage into the enchanting tapestry of 1959, a year etched with the vivid hues of change, ambition, and the symphony of a generation in transition. Whether you were an eyewitness to the era's pivotal moments or have been enthralled by its legends, this book serves as a heartfelt homage to the enduring essence of a bygone time.

Immerse yourself in the spellbinding stories, cultural portraits, and cherished recollections that compose the essence of 1959. Within these pages, we invite you to rediscover the profound resonance and sentimentality interwoven into the very soul of this remarkable epoch.

Hope each chapter kindle a sense of solace, ignite a spark of inspiration, and foster a profound connection to the vibrant narratives that continue to shape our collective history. Join us in this expedition through 1959, where the past dances to life, and the spirit of an era whispers its timeless ballads."

Warmest regards,
Edward Art Lab

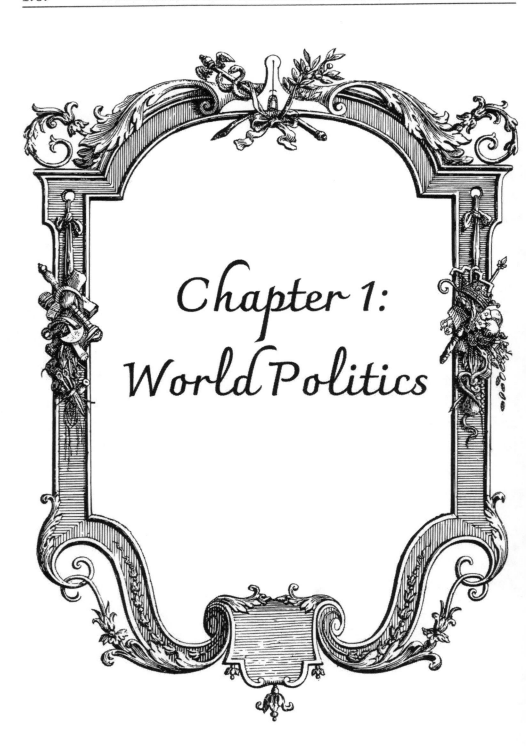

Chapter 1: World Politics

In 1959, the world was still heavily influenced by the aftermath of World War II, with the Cold War between the United States and the Soviet Union continuing to shape global politics. Some key events and developments in world politics during 1959:

1. Remarkable political events of '59

Fidel Castro came to power in Cuba after the Revolution

Fidel Castro's ascension to power in Cuba marked a pivotal moment in the country's history, leading to the establishment of a socialist government and significantly altering the geopolitical dynamics of the region. Castro's revolutionary zeal and anti-imperialist stance led to strained relations with the United States, setting the stage for decades of tension and conflict.

Soviet Union - Kitchen Debate

On July 24, United States Vice President Richard Nixon and the Soviet Union's Premier Nikita Khrushchev engaged in an impromptu debate. The exchange took place at a U.S. trade show being held in Moscow. Known as the "Kitchen Debate," the two leaders argued the merits of capitalism and communism while standing in a model of a modern kitchen displayed for the American National Exhibition. The whole encounter was filmed by the American press and aired in both nations.

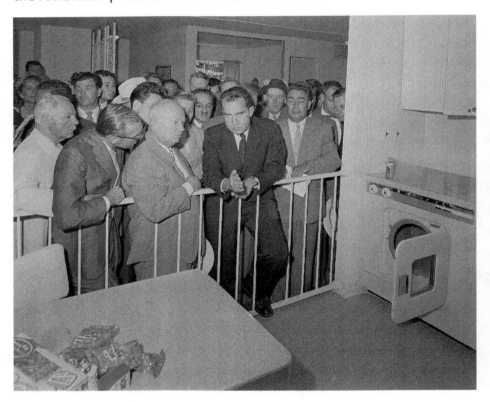

The debate between United States Vice President Richard Nixon and Soviet Union's Premier Nikita Khrushchev was a significant event during the Cold War, highlighting the tensions and ideological differences between the two superpowers.

The Dalai Lama and tens of thousands of Tibetans flee to India

In March, China's forceful invasion of Tibet prompted an unparalleled exodus as the revered spiritual leader, the Dalai Lama, and numerous Tibetans embarked on a perilous journey to seek refuge across the Indian border. This poignant moment encapsulated the enduring struggle of the Tibetan people for autonomy and sovereignty, as they grappled with the imminent threat to their cultural and religious heritage.

United States - Hawaii became the 50th state

In summer of 1959, Hawaii was officially inducted into the illustrious family of the United States as its 50th state. The momentous occasion symbolized a harmonious fusion of tradition and modernity, as the island's rich Polynesian heritage intertwined seamlessly with the dynamic spirit of the American dream.

United States - Canada - St. Lawrence Seaway is completed

This groundbreaking infrastructure achievement not only solidified the bond between the United States and Canada but also forged a path for increased collaboration and mutual prosperity. It propelled the development of key industries and bolstered the competitiveness of businesses, paving the way for a new era of international trade and cooperation. The St. Lawrence Seaway remains an enduring symbol of cross-border partnership and a testament to the enduring power of human innovation in shaping the modern world.

The Antarctic Treaty

In 1959, a groundbreaking moment of international cooperation and environmental stewardship unfolded in Washington as twelve nations came together to sign the Antarctic Treaty. This historic agreement marked a significant milestone in the collective efforts to preserve one of the Earth's most pristine and delicate ecosystems, the Antarctic continent.

2. Major World Political Leaders in 1959

Dwight D. Eisenhower

Serving as the President of the United States, Eisenhower played a crucial role in shaping U.S. foreign policy during the height of the Cold War. His presidency was characterized by a focus on international diplomacy, including efforts to ease tensions with the Soviet Union and promote peace and stability in a rapidly changing global landscape.

Harold Macmillan

The Prime Minister of the United Kingdom, Macmillan, played a key role in advancing British foreign policy, including efforts to address the challenges of decolonization and the United Kingdom's changing role in the global political landscape. He also oversaw significant domestic reforms, contributing to the shaping of modern British society.

Sir Robert Menzies

Menzies, the Prime Minister of Australia, was known for his long tenure and his efforts in strengthening Australia's economy and global relations. He played a key role in promoting the country's interests on the international stage, particularly during the Cold War era.

Juscelino Kubitschek

As the President of Brazil, Kubitschek is remembered for his ambitious development initiatives, including the construction of the new capital city, Brasília. His administration focused on modernizing Brazil's infrastructure and fostering economic growth, leaving a lasting legacy in the country's urban development.

John Diefenbaker

The Prime Minister of Canada, Diefenbaker, played a significant role in advancing human rights and enacting progressive legislation, including the Canadian Bill of Rights. His leadership emphasized a commitment to democratic principles and social justice, contributing to Canada's evolving political landscape.

Liu Shaoqi

Holding the position of Chairman of the People's Republic of China, Liu Shaoqi was instrumental in shaping China's political landscape during a crucial period of the country's history. His leadership and contributions were particularly significant during the early years of the People's Republic of China.

Charles de Gaulle

De Gaulle, who became the President of France in 1959, was a towering figure in French politics, known for his leadership during World War II and his subsequent efforts in reshaping France's role in global affairs. He was a driving force in establishing the Fifth Republic and played a key role in promoting France's independence and sovereignty on the world stage.

Nikita Khrushchev

As the First Secretary of the Central Committee of the Communist Party of the Soviet Union, Khrushchev led the Soviet Union during a period of significant political and ideological upheaval, including the de-Stalinization campaign and the Cuban Missile Crisis. His tenure was marked by efforts to reform the Soviet political system and promote a thaw in the Cold War tensions.

Konrad Adenauer

As the Chancellor of Germany, Adenauer played a pivotal role in the reconstruction of post-war Germany and in strengthening the country's ties with Western nations. His leadership was instrumental in the economic and political revitalization of West Germany during the early years of the Cold War.

Adolfo Ruiz Cortines

Adolfo Ruiz Cortines, who served as the President of Mexico until November 30, 1958, made significant contributions to the country's social and economic development during his presidency. Ruiz Cortines, a reform-minded leader, implemented various policies that sought to address pressing social issues and promote economic growth.

Activity: Historical Triava Quiz
Test Your Knowledge of 1959

Are you ready to challenge your knowledge of the significant events and key figures of 1959? Here's a historical trivia quiz to test your knowledge of the events and leaders in 1959:

1. Which country became the 50th state of the United States in 1959?
a) Alaska
b) Hawaii
c) Puerto Rico
d) Guam

2. Who was the iconic leader who fled to India along with thousands of Tibetans following China's invasion of Tibet in 1959?
a) Mahatma Gandhi
b) Dalai Lama
c) Mao Zedong
d) Ho Chi Minh

3. Which international treaty was signed in 1959, aimed at preserving Antarctica as a zone of peace and scientific research?
a) Geneva Convention
b) Antarctica Protection Treaty
c) Antarctic Conservation Act
d) Antarctic Treaty System

4. What significant transnational infrastructure project was completed in 1959, connecting the United States and Canada relationship?
a) Panama Canal
b) Suez Canal
c) St. Lawrence Seaway
d) Erie Canal

5. Who was the leader of the Soviet Union as the First Secretary of the Central Committee of the Communist Party of the Soviet Union in 1959?
a) Mikhail Gorbachev
b) Vladimir Lenin
c) Joseph Stalin
d) Nikita Khrushchev

6. Who assumed the presidency of France in 1959, leading the country during a critical period of political transformation and asserting its global independence?
a) Charles de Gaulle
b) Francois Mitterrand
c) Emmanuel Macron
d) Nicolas Sarkozy

7. Who served as the Prime Minister of India in 1959, playing a crucial role in shaping the country's foreign policy and promoting the principles of democracy and secularism?
a) Indira Gandhi
b) Rajiv Gandhi
c) Jawaharlal Nehru
d) Narendra Modi

8. Who was the President of the United States in 1959, overseeing critical foreign policy decisions during the height of the Cold War and emphasizing international diplomacy to ease tensions with the Soviet Union?
a) John F. Kennedy
b) Dwight D. Eisenhower
c) Harry S. Truman
d) Franklin D. Roosevelt

Chapter 2:
Entertainment in 1959

Entertainment in 1959 saw the continuation of various trends in film, music, and television, with several notable releases and developments.

Films and Prestigious Film Awards

In the vibrant tapestry of 1959's cinematic landscape, a constellation of legendary films illuminated the silver screen, forever shaping the course of cinema history.

1. Memorable Films of '59
Ben-Hur

William Wyler's epic masterpiece "Ben-Hur" continues to mesmerize audiences with its grandeur and spectacle, bringing to life a sweeping tale of betrayal, redemption, and courage set against the backdrop of ancient Rome. The film's breathtaking chariot race sequence and powerful performances, notably Charlton Heston's portrayal of the titular character, have solidified its place as a timeless cinematic classic.

Some Like It Hot

  Billy Wilder's comedic gem "Some Like It Hot" remains a perennial favorite, renowned for its witty dialogue, charismatic performances, and the magnetic presence of Marilyn Monroe. The film's clever humor and playful exploration of gender dynamics have secured its reputation as one of the most beloved and enduring comedies in the history of cinema.

Anatomy of a Murder

Otto Preminger's gripping courtroom drama "Anatomy of a Murder" captivated audiences with its nuanced exploration of a sensational murder trial, expertly portrayed by a stellar cast led by James Stewart. The film's complex character dynamics, sharp dialogue, and thought-provoking examination of justice and morality have cemented its status as a classic of the genre.

North by Northwest

Directed by Alfred Hitchcock, this suspenseful thriller, starring Cary Grant and Eva Marie Saint, enthralled audiences with its masterful blend of mystery, intrigue, and adventure, featuring iconic sequences such as the famous crop-duster chase scene and the climactic Mount Rushmore finale.

Sleeping Beauty

Produced by Walt Disney, this animated fairy tale film enchanted audiences with its breathtaking animation, memorable characters, and a captivating retelling of the classic story, showcasing Disney's signature artistry and imaginative storytelling.

It captivated audiences of all ages for generations.

2. Prestigious Film Awards

In 1959, several prestigious film awards were presented, honoring the outstanding achievements in the film industry during that year. Some of the notable awards included:

Academy Awards (Oscars)

The 31st Academy Awards ceremony was held on April 6, 1959, at the Pantages Theatre in Hollywood, California.

Best Picture:	**Best Director:**
"Gigi"	Vincente Minnelli for "Gigi"

Best Actor:	**Best Actress:**
David Niven for "Separate Tables"	Susan Hayward for "I Want to Live!"

Golden Globe Awards

The 16th Golden Globe Awards took place on March 6, 1959. Some of the notable winners were:

Best Motion Picture - Drama: **Best Motion Picture - Musical or Comedy:**
"The Defiant Ones"   *"Gigi"*

Best Director:
Vincente Minnelli for "Gigi"

Best Actor - Drama: **Best Actress - Drama:**
David Niven for "Separate Tables"   Susan Hayward for "I Want to Live!"

Best Actor - Musical or Comedy:
Danny Kaye for "Me and the Colonel"

Best Actress - Musical or Comedy:
Rosalind Russell for "Auntie Mame"

Cannes Film Festival

The 12th Cannes Film Festival was held from April 30 to May 15, 1959. The top prize, the Palme d'Or, was awarded to the French film "Orfeu Negro" (Black Orpheus) directed by Marcel Camus.

Music: Top Songs and Awards

1. Top songs

Some significant musical highlights from that year:

Mack the Knife

"Mack the Knife" by Bobby Darin is indeed one of the most iconic and enduring songs from 1959. It was a significant hit during that year and has since become a timeless classic, celebrated for its infectious melody and Darin's captivating performance. The song's catchy tune, coupled with its memorable lyrics and "Mack the Knife" has continued to resonate with audiences across generations, solidifying its place as one of the standout tracks of the 20th century.

The Battle of New Orleans

"The Battle of New Orleans" by Johnny Horton is a historically significant song that achieved great success in 1959. It narrates the story of the Battle of New Orleans, a crucial event during the War of 1812 between the United States and the British Empire. The song's narrative quality, combined with Horton's distinctive voice and the catchy melody, made it a standout hit during its time.

"The Battle of New Orleans" was honored with the Grammy Award for Song of the Year in 1960.

Venus

"Venus" by Frankie Avalon is a classic pop song that enjoyed immense popularity in 1959. It captivated audiences with its catchy melody and Avalon's smooth vocals, ultimately becoming one of the defining hits of the late 1950s. The song's infectious rhythm and romantic lyrics resonated with listeners, contributing to its widespread success and enduring appeal.

Lonely Boy

This emotionally resonant song by Paul Anka was well-received in 1959 and has since become a timeless classic, known for its heartfelt lyrics and Anka's soulful performance. "Lonely Boy" remains a cherished piece of music history, embodying the essence of timeless and heartfelt songwriting.

Stagger Lee

"Stagger Lee" by Lloyd Price was a significant R&B hit in 1959 that reached the top of the Billboard Hot 100 chart, showcasing Price's prowess as a musician and solidifying his place in music history. The song's infectious rhythm, energetic vocals, and compelling narrative captivated audiences, making it one of the standout tracks of the late 1950s.

Personality

"Personality" by Lloyd Price was another notable hit in 1959 that further solidified Price's prominence in the music industry. The song, with its infectious rhythm and catchy lyrics, exemplified Price's versatility and musical talent, showcasing his ability to deliver engaging and memorable performances that resonated with a wide audience.

Kansas City

"Kansas City" by Wilbert Harrison was a highly successful rhythm and blues song in 1959 that garnered widespread acclaim for its infectious beat and lively energy. The song's catchy rhythm, spirited vocals, and vibrant musical arrangement made it a standout hit of the late 1950s, capturing the attention of audiences and establishing itself as a classic in the R&B genre.

2. Renowned singers of '59

1959 saw the continued prominence of several renowned singers, each making significant contributions to the music industry. Some of the noteworthy singers during that period were:

Elvis Presley

The King of Rock and Roll, Elvis Presley, continued to be a dominant force in the music industry in 1959, with several successful releases and continued popularity among fans worldwide.

Paul Anka

Paul Anka, the Canadian-American singer and songwriter, indeed enjoyed significant success in 1959, consolidating his position as a prominent figure in the world of popular music. Anka's hits, including "Diana" and "Lonely Boy," were particularly instrumental in his rise to fame during this period. These songs showcased Anka's vocal talent and songwriting abilities, capturing the hearts of audiences worldwide with their memorable melodies and relatable lyrics.

The Platters

The Platters were an influential vocal group that maintained their popularity and musical significance in 1959. Known for their distinctive vocal harmonies and classic hits like "Only You" and "The Great Pretender," The Platters were at the forefront of the R&B and doo-wop music scenes during the late 1950s.

Doris Day

Doris Day is known for her versatile singing and acting career. Her musical contributions, characterized by her emotive vocal range and lively performances, resonated with audiences, solidifying her position as one of the leading female singers of the era.

Frank Sinatra

Frank Sinatra, the legendary American singer and actor, indeed maintained his iconic status in 1959, further solidifying his position as one of the most influential and celebrated artists of the 20th century. Known for his exceptional vocal talent, charismatic stage presence, and remarkable contributions to the realms of popular music and film, Sinatra remained a dominant figure in the entertainment industry during this period.

Connie Francis

Connie Francis, with her versatile vocal range and charismatic performances, continued to make a significant impact in the music industry in 1959. Known for her string of successful hits such as "Who's Sorry Now" and "Lipstick on Your Collar," Francis solidified her position as one of the leading female vocalists of the era, captivating audiences with her emotive and dynamic musical style.

Jim Reeves

Country music star Jim Reeves, known for hits like "He'll Have to Go" and "Four Walls," was a prominent figure in the country music scene in 1959.

Cliff Richard

He is the British singer. Known for hits such as "Living Doll" and "Travellin' Light," experienced a rise to prominence in the late 1950s and continued to solidify his position as a prominent musical figure in 1959. hE highlighted his significant influence on the development of British rock and pop music, solidifying his place as one of the most celebrated and enduring musical talents in the history of British popular music.

Activity: Let's guess name of song from the lyrics

1. "Oh, the shark, babe, has such teeth, dear And he shows them pearly white".

   ....

2. "In 1814 we took a little trip, along with Colonel Jackson down the mighty Mississip..."

   ....

3. "I've got everything, you could think of, but all I want, is someone to love..."

   ....

4. "Goddess on the mountain topurning like a silver flame..."

   ....

Chapter 3: Art and Literature in 1959

In 1959, the world of art and literature experienced various notable developments, including significant works, movements, and achievements across different forms of artistic expression.

Popular books published in 1959

1. The Haunting of Hill House

"The Haunting of Hill House" is a classic supernatural horror novel written by Shirley Jackson. First published in 1959, the novel is widely regarded as one of the best literary ghost stories of the 20th century. It has since become a seminal work in the horror genre, renowned for its atmospheric tension, psychological depth, and exploration of the supernatural.

2. Flowers for Algernon

Be a poignant and thought-provoking science fiction novel written by Daniel Keyes. It was first published as a short story in 1959 and later expanded into a full novel in 1966. The story revolves around Charlie Gordon, a mentally disabled man who undergoes an experimental surgical procedure to increase his intelligence.

3. The Tin Drum

"The Tin Drum" by Günter Grass is a significant and influential novel in 1959. The story is set in Danzig and spans the period from the pre-World War II era through the post-war years, providing a vivid portrayal of the social and political climate during the rise of Nazi Germany and the subsequent aftermath of the war. It widespread critical acclaim and a lasting place in the canon of modern literary masterpieces.

4. The Sirens of Titan

"The Sirens of Titan" by Kurt Vonnegut: Kurt Vonnegut's second novel, "The Sirens of Titan," is a satirical science fiction work that explores themes of free will, fate, and the purpose of human existence. The story follows the journey of Malachi Constant as he is manipulated by a cosmic force.

5. Starship Troopers

"Starship Troopers" is a military science fiction novel written by Robert A. Heinlein. "Starship Troopers" has become a seminal work in the science fiction genre, known for its exploration of themes related to military service and societal values. It has inspired numerous adaptations, including a film adaptation in 1997, further solidifying its place in popular culture and its enduring influence on the realm of science fiction literature.

6. A Separate Peace

"A Separate Peace" by John Knowles is indeed a classic coming-of-age novel that delves into the complexities of friendship, rivalry, and the loss of innocence. Set in a fictional New England preparatory school during World War II. The novel's enduring popularity and its poignant portrayal of the complexities of human relationships and the universal struggles of growing up have contributed to its status as a cherished and thought-provoking piece of literature.

Arts in 1959

Some of the notable events and influential figures in the arts during this period include:

The National Museum of Western Art was indeed established in Tokyo, Japan, on June 10, 1959. The museum was designed by the renowned Swiss-French architect Le Corbusier and is known for its collection of Western art, including works by prominent European artists from various periods. The museum's establishment marked a significant milestone in Japan's cultural landscape, providing a platform for the exhibition and appreciation of Western art in the country.

The first public "**Happening**," titled "Eighteen Happenings in Six Parts," was indeed presented by the American artist Allan Kaprow at the Reuben Gallery in New York City in the fall of 1959. This event marked a significant moment in the development of performance art, as it incorporated elements of visual art, theater, and experimental techniques, challenging traditional boundaries and inviting audience participation.

Allan Kaprow, Eighteen Happenings in Six Parts, Reuban Gallery, New York, 1959.

The 1959 Archibald Prize.

In 1959, William Dobell was awarded the Archibald Prize for his portrait of Dr. Edward MacMahon. Dobell, an esteemed Australian portrait and landscape artist, gained recognition for his exceptional skill in capturing the likeness and character of his subjects.

William Dobell for "Dr Edward MacMahon"
Winner of the Archibald Prize 1959

Influential figures in the arts in 1959

Abstract Expressionism and Pop Art: The art world witnessed the continuation of Abstract Expressionism and the rise of Pop Art, with artists like Andy Warhol gaining recognition for their groundbreaking work.

"Ice Cream Dessert" by Andy Warhol , Pop Art

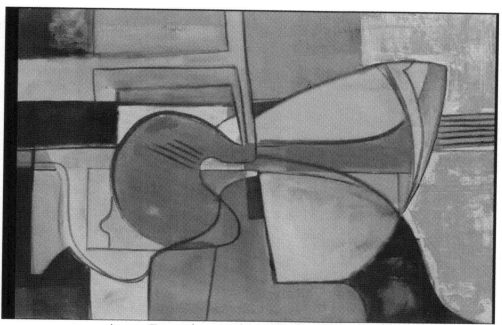

Irene Zevon's art, Abstract Expressionism

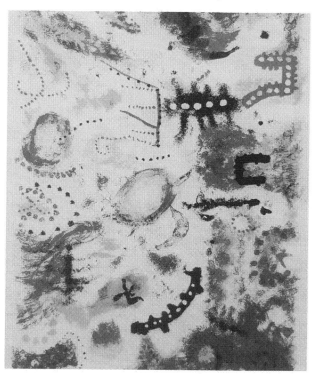

By Tadashi Nakayama

Avant-Garde Movements

Avant-garde movements, characterized by experimental and innovative approaches to art, continued to push the boundaries of artistic expression, with artists exploring new forms and concepts.

"Woman with cloth" by Vera Grigorenko

Sculpture

Notable sculptors such as Henry Moore and Alexander Calder continued to create significant works that captured the imagination of the art world.

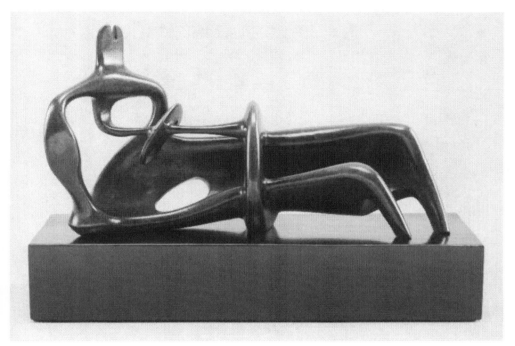

Activity: Crossword Puzzle
Test your Knowledge in 1959

Are your ready to challenge your knowledge of literature and art in 1959?

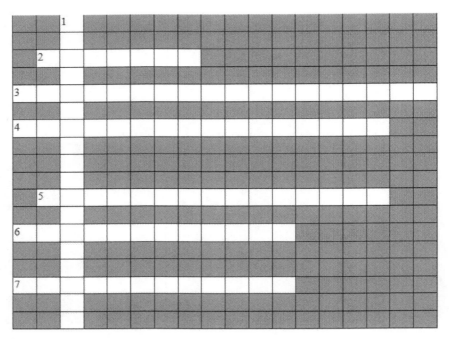

ACROSS

2. Art movement that gained prominence during the 1950s, known for their distinct approaches to artistic expression.

3. Shirley Jackson's eerie novel about a haunted mansion.

4. John Knowles' coming-of-age novel set in a prep school during World War II.

5. A prestigious Australian art award won by William Dobell in 1959.

6. Important literary works and artistic trends during the late 1950s were influenced by these avant-garde movements.

7. Gunter Grass' notable work exploring the rise of Nazism in Germany.

KEYWORD:

1_____

Enjoy solving the crossword puzzle!

Chapter 4: Sports in 1959 A Journey Through the World

In 1959, the world of sports witnessed various significant events and achievements across different athletic disciplines. Some of the notable occurrences in the realm of sports

Football

The 1959, **NFL Championship Game** was won by the **Baltimore Colts**, who defeated the New York Giants in a thrilling and historic match. The Colts' victory in the championship game solidified their status as one of the prominent teams in the National Football League during that era and contributed to the team's enduring legacy in the realm of professional football.

Baltimore Colts team

Baseball

In 1959, the Los Angeles Dodgers emerged victorious in the World Series of Major League Baseball, solidifying their place as one of the dominant teams in the league during that era. The Dodgers' success in the World Series highlighted their exceptional skill and teamwork, showcasing their ability to compete at the highest level of professional baseball.

Los Angeles Dodgers Roster

Boxing

June 26 – in New York City, Ingemar Johansson scored a 3rd-round TKO over Floyd Patterson to win the World Heavyweight Championship.

Golf

The U.S. Open in golf was won by Billy Casper, and the British Open was won by Gary Player.

Billy Casper   *Gary Player*

Ice Hockey

In 1959, the Montreal Canadiens emerged victorious in the Stanley Cup, defeating the Toronto Maple Leafs by winning the series 4 games to 1.

At the World Hockey Championship, the men's championship was secured by the Belleville McFarlands from Canada.

Basketball

In the 1959 FIBA World Championship, the Brazilian national basketball team achieved a historic victory, securing the title of World Champion.

Horse Racing

The 113th renewal of the **Grand National horse race** that took place at Aintree Racecourse near Liverpool, on 21 March. The Grand National steeplechase was won by the horse **Oxo**

Roddy Owen rode the winning horse to victory in the **Cheltenham Gold Cup**, a renowned steeplechase event in the United Kingdom.

Tennis

The Wimbledon Championships:

Alex Olmedo won in
the men's singles

Maria Bueno won in
the women's singles

The French Open:

Nicola Pietrangeli won
in the men's singles

Christine Truman won
in the women's singles

The US Open:

Neale Fraser in
The men's singles

Maria Bueno in
in the women's singles

Activity: Test Your Knowledge of 1959 Sports History

Enjoy the multiple-choice quiz and see how well you remember the exciting sports history of 1959!

1. Who won the Men's Singles title at the Wimbledon Championships in 1959?
a) Alex Olmedo
b) Neale Fraser
c) Nicola Pietrangeli
d) Rod Laver

2. Which team emerged as the Stanley Cup winner in 1959?
a) Detroit Red Wings
b) Montreal Canadiens
c) Toronto Maple Leafs
d) Chicago Blackhawks

3. Who won the World Series in Major League Baseball in 1959?
a) New York Yankees
b) Los Angeles Dodgers
c) Boston Red Sox
d) San Francisco Giants

4. Which Brazilian athlete was the Men's Singles champion at the French Open in 1959?
a) Gustavo Kuerten
b) Maria Bueno
c) Gustavo Poyet
d) Nicola Pietrangeli

5. Who was the winner of the 1959 NFL Championship Game?
a) Baltimore Colts
b) New York Giants
c) Green Bay Packers
d) Chicago Bears

6. Which horse won the Grand National in 1959?
a) Red Rum
b) Oxo
c) L'Escargot
d) Manifesto

7. Who won the World Hockey Championship for men in 1959?
a) Canada
b) United States
c) Soviet Union
d) Sweden

8. Who was the winner of the 1959 FIBA World Championship in basketball?
a) United States
b) Brazil
c) Soviet Union
d) Argentina

Coloring Time

Chapter 5:
Fashion, and Popular Leisure Activities

Fashion

Fashion in 1959 was influenced by the evolving cultural and social changes of the time. The late 1950s marked a transition from the post-war austerity to a more vibrant and glamorous era.

Women's fashion

New Silhouettes

The prevalent silhouette for women's fashion in 1959 featured a continuation of the fitted bodice and a full, flared skirt, often accentuated with petticoats or crinolines. The hourglass figure was emphasized, highlighting the waist and creating a feminine and elegant look.

Bell Shaped Skirt Dress

The bell-shaped skirt dress, a prominent fashion trend in the 1950s, featured a distinctively flared or full skirt that resembled the shape of a bell.

Accessories

In 1959, various accessories played a significant role in completing the polished and refined look of women.

Hats: Women commonly wore a variety of hat styles in 1959, including pillbox hats, cloche hats, and wide-brimmed sun hats. These hats added a touch of sophistication and glamour to their outfits, enhancing the overall elegance of their appearance.

Gloves: Gloves were a staple accessory, often made of fine fabrics such as silk, satin, or kid leather. Women wore gloves that matched or complemented their outfits, further accentuating their refined and well-coordinated ensembles.

Handbags: Women in 1959 often carried structured handbags that emphasized both style and functionality. Common styles included boxy and structured handbags, often made of materials such as leather, vinyl, or fabric. These handbags featured top handles or short straps and were often adorned with simple, understated hardware, reflecting the classic and refined aesthetic of the era.

Accessories

Scarves: Women commonly wore scarves, which added a touch of sophistication and versatility to their outfits. Silk scarves, in particular, were popular, and women styled them in various ways to complement their ensembles.

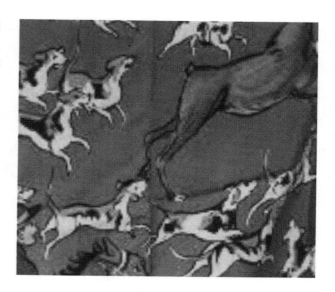

Shoes: Women's shoes in 1959 were characterized by classic and feminine designs, with popular choices including low-heeled pumps, kitten heels, and ballet flats. These shoes were often made of high-quality materials such as leather or suede, providing both style and comfort for various occasions..

Belts: Women's belts were often slim and accentuated their waists

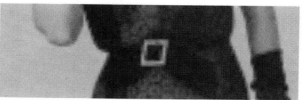

Jewelry

Women often wore jewelry such as pearls, simple necklaces, and earrings, which added a subtle yet elegant touch to their overall look.

Hairstyles

Hairstyles for women with popular choices include victory rolls, short curls, and the classic pageboy haircut. Often adorned with hair accessories such as decorative pins, headbands, and bows, adding a playful and feminine element to their looks.

Fashion for Men in 1959
Tailored Suits

uits were a staple of men's fashion in 1959, with a focus on tailored and well-fitted designs. Two-piece and three-piece suits in neutral colors such as gray, navy, and black were popular, exuding a timeless and polished look.

Shirts: Dress shirts were typically white or light-colored, with long sleeves and pointed collars. These shirts were often worn with ties, contributing to a formal and sophisticated appearance.

Trousers: Men's trousers were high-waisted and often featured a straight or slightly tapered leg. They were usually tailored to fit well and were commonly worn with a belt to complete the polished look.

Popular Leisure Activities

Several popular toys and leisure activities captured the imagination of children and families, reflecting the era's cultural and technological influences. Some of the notable toys and leisure activities from 1959 included:

The Barbie Doll quickly became a beloved and influential cultural icon, shaping the way children played and interacted with toys.

Activity: Let's draw a picture of "fashion of 1959"

Enjoy your artistic exploration of the fashion of 1959!

Chapter 6: Technological Advancements and Innovation

Technological events

In 1959, the world witnessed a series of groundbreaking technological advancements and innovations that significantly influenced various sectors and shaped the trajectory of progress.

Boeing 707 Jet Airliner

The introduction of the Boeing 707 jet airliner revolutionized commercial air travel, reducing transatlantic flight times by eight hours and marking the beginning of the modern era of jet-powered aviation.

Space Exploration Milestones

Several significant achievements were made in space exploration, including the USSR's Luna 2, the first human-made object to crash onto the Moon, and Luna 3, which captured and transmitted the first photographs of the far side of the Moon. Additionally, the US satellite Explorer 6 took the first pictures of Earth from space.

USSR's Luna 2

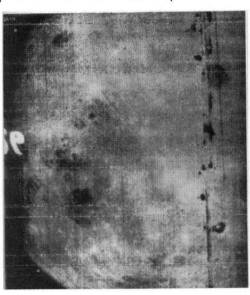

Luna 3's Image From the Dark Side

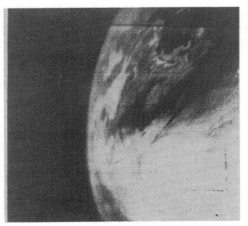

First image of Earth from orbit
taken by Explorer VI on August 14, 1959

The shipment of the transistor-based IBM 1401 mainframe

In 1959, IBM achieved a significant milestone in computing technology with the shipment of the transistor-based IBM 1401 mainframe. It was one of the company's early transistorized computers, representing a shift away from vacuum tube-based systems and signaling the beginning of a new era in computer technology.

Xerox 914- The first commercial copier

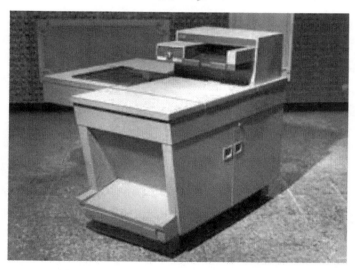

Xerox Corporation made history by launching the first commercial copier, known as the Xerox 914. The Xerox 914 marked a significant turning point in the history of office automation, ushering in a new era of photocopying technology that would eventually become an indispensable tool for the future.

Development of the Hovercraft

The successful testing of the full-size hovercraft, the SR-N1 by Sir Christopher Cockerell, opened up new possibilities for innovative transportation solutions, both over land and water.

M1 Motorway

The opening of the first section of the M1 Motorway in the United Kingdom, connecting London to Birmingham, signaled a new era of efficient and modern transportation infrastructure, paving the way for further development of the country's road network.

US Weather Station in Space

The United States launched its first weather station into space, marking a significant milestone in space technology and the study of meteorological phenomena from orbit.

QANTAS and Boeing 707

QANTAS, the Australian airline, introduced the Boeing 707 on its Sydney-San Francisco route, marking the first transpacific service flown by a jet. This event marked a significant advancement in international air travel.

De Beers manufactures a synthetic Diamond

De Beers, the renowned diamond company, accomplished a notable feat by manufacturing a synthetic diamond. This milestone marked a significant development in the field of gemstone production, showcasing the potential for creating diamonds through artificial means

Microchip USA by Jack Kilby

The microchip was invented in the USA by Jack Kilby, laying the groundwork for the development of integrated circuits and marking a pivotal advancement in the field of electronic technology.

The Automobiles of 1959

In 1959, reached the climax of its grand era in automotive design. The stylists reached the outer limits of what could be accomplished with fins and chrome, crafting some of the most memorable cars that havebeen ever produced.

Chevrolet El Camino

The first generation of the Chevrolet El Camino, which combined the features of a car with the utility of a pickup truck, was introduced in 1959, setting the stage for the later popularity of this unique vehicle type.

• Austin Mini

On August 26, 1959, the Austin/Morris Mini was introduced in the United Kindom. This groundbreaking layout significantly influenced the development of subsequent vehicles, contributing to advancements in automotive engineering and design that continue to resonate in the industry to this day.

Ford Galaxie

The Ford Galaxie series, known for its stylish design and powerful V8 engines, was well-received by consumers in 1959. It marked a significant milestone for Ford in the full-size car segment.

Pontiac Bonneville

The Pontiac Bonneville, known for its sleek styling and powerful performance, captured the essence of American muscle cars during this era, appealing to consumers seeking both style and speed.

Activity:
Test Your Knowledge of Technology in 1959

"Welcome to the Milestone Fill-in activity! In this engaging challenge, you'll have the opportunity to fill-in Technological events with their corresponding significant milestones. Each event represents a remarkable achievement in various fields.

1) Major breakthrough in space exploration

_____

2) Landmark in the aviation industry

_____

3) The first commercial copier

_____

4) Revolutionary advancement in transportation

_____

5) Notable development in the diamond industry

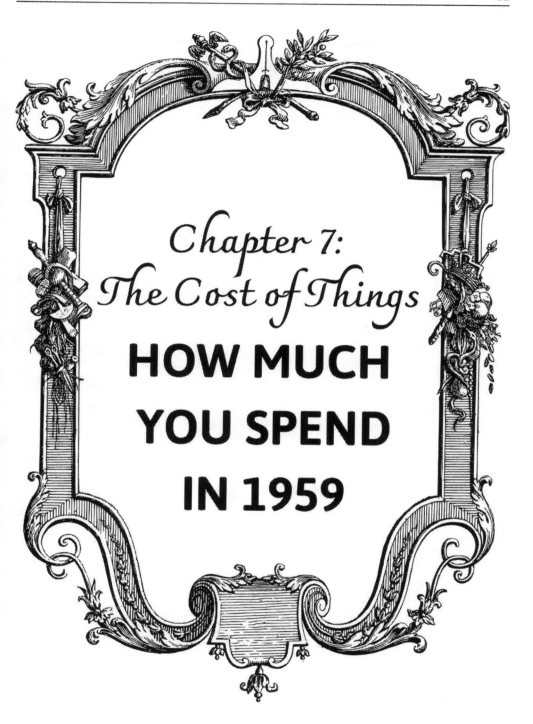

Chapter 7:
The Cost of Things
HOW MUCH YOU SPEND IN 1959

Cost of Living in 1959

- *Average Cost of new house $12,400.00*
- *Average wages per year $5,600.00*
- Average Rent $97.00 per month

Cost of Living in 1959
- *Cost of Gas $2.55 per gallon*

- *Average Cost New Car $2,250.00*

Cost of Living in 1959
Food

- *Granulated Sugar: $9 for 10 pounds*
- *Vitamin D Milk: $10.28*
- *Ground Coffee: $9.67 per pound*
- *Bacon: $6.41 per pound*
- *Eggs: $2.95 per dozen*
- *Fresh Ground Hamburger: $5.91 per pound*
- *Fresh Baked Bread: $2.04 per loaf*

Activity: How the life changed

Write your cost of living monthly

SHOPPING LIST

☐	☐
☐	☐
☐	☐
☐	☐
☐	☐
☐	☐
☐	☐
☐	☐
☐	☐
☐	☐
☐	☐
☐	☐
☐	☐
☐	☐
☐	☐
☐	☐
☐	☐

Activity: How the life changed

Comparing prices from 1959 with the cost of similar items in the present day. Reflect on the changes in consumer behavior

Chapter 8:

Births in 1959

Several notable individuals were born in 1959 across various fields, including politics, entertainment, and sports. Here are some famous births from that year:

1. Jason Alexander

- Date of Birth: September 23rd, 1959

Jason Alexander is celebrated for his significant contributions to the entertainment industry, particularly for his iconic portrayal of the character George Costanza in the critically acclaimed television sitcom "Seinfeld." His remarkable comedic timing and acting prowess have left a lasting mark on popular culture.

2. Fred Couples

- Date of Birth: October 3rd, 1959

Fred Couples is renowned for his exceptional contributions to the sport of golf, having achieved numerous victories on both the PGA Tour and the PGA Champions Tour. His skill, grace, and influential presence on the golf course have solidified his status as one of the most respected and admired professional golfers of his time.

3. Simon Cowell

- Date of Birth: October 7th, 1959

Simon Cowell has made significant contributions to the music industry and television, gaining widespread recognition as a sharp-witted and discerning judge on popular talent shows such as "American Idol" and "The X Factor." His influence on the discovery and development of new musical talents has shaped the modern entertainment landscape.

4. Hugh Laurie

- Date of Birth: June 11th, 1959

Hugh Laurie has left a notable legacy in the entertainment industry, known for his exceptional acting skills showcased in various critically acclaimed television series and films. His versatile performances, particularly in the medical drama series "House," have earned him widespread acclaim and admiration from audiences and critics alike.

5. Sean Bean

- Date of Birth: April 17th, 1959

Sean Bean has made significant contributions to the world of entertainment through his captivating performances in various films and television shows, earning critical acclaim for his versatile acting abilities and memorable portrayals of complex and multifaceted characters.

6. Emma Thompson

- Date of Birth: April 15th, 1959

Emma Thompson is esteemed for her remarkable contributions to the film industry, known for her exceptional acting talent and dedication to her craft. Her versatile performances in a diverse range of films have earned her critical acclaim and numerous awards, solidifying her status as one of the most respected and influential actresses of her generation.

7. Allison Janney

- Date of Birth: November 19th, 1959

Allison Janney has made notable contributions to the world of entertainment through her versatile and compelling performances in various films and television shows. Her award-winning portrayal of C.J. Cregg in the television series "The West Wing" and her dynamic roles in other projects have garnered widespread acclaim and accolades.

8. Mike Pence

- Date of Birth: June 7th, 1959

Mike Pence has made substantial contributions to the political landscape, serving as the 48th Vice President of the United States from 2017 to 2021 and holding various positions in government throughout his career. His contributions to American politics have shaped policies and discussions on various issues, leaving a notable impact on the country's political history.

Activity: "Profiles in Achievement: The Noteworthy Births of 1959"

Let's check your knowledge of famous births of 1959. Choose the correct answer (a, b, c, d) for each question.

1. Who was born on September 23rd, 1959, in Newark, NJ?

a) Jason Alexander

b) Fred Couples

c) Simon Cowell

d) Hugh Laurie

2. Which American politician served as the 48th Vice President of the United States from 2017 to 2021 and was previously the governor of Indiana?

a) Jason Alexander

b) Fred Couples

c) Simon Cowell

d) Mike Pence

3. Who is best known for portraying the character George Costanza in the popular television series "Seinfeld"?

a) Jason Alexander

b) Fred Couples

c) Simon Cowell

d) Hugh Laurie

4. Which American professional golfer won the Masters Tournament in 1992 and has had a successful career in the world of golf?
a) Jason Alexander
b) Fred Couples
c) Simon Cowell
d) Hugh Laurie

5. Who gained international fame as a judge on television talent competition shows like "American Idol" and "The X Factor" for his blunt and controversial criticisms?
a) Jason Alexander
b) Fred Couples
c) Simon Cowell
d) Hugh Laurie

6. Who was born on November 19th, 1959, in Boston, MA?
a) Jason Alexander
b) Fred Couples
c) Simon Cowell
d) Allison Janney

7. Who is known for his versatile roles in both heroic and villainous characters, including his portrayal of Boromir in "The Lord of the Rings" film trilogy?
a) Jason Alexander
b) Fred Couples
c) Simon Cowell
d) Sean Bean

Do you know Celebrities Born in 1959?

_____

_____

_____

_____

_____

_____

_____

_____

_____

_____

_____

_____

_____

_____

_____

_____

_____

_____

_____

_____

_____

_____

We have heartfelt thank-you gifts for you

As a token of our appreciation for joining us on this historical journey through 1959, we've included a set of cards and stamps inspired by the year of 1959. These cards are your canvas to capture the essence of the past. We encourage you to use them as inspiration for creating your own unique cards, sharing your perspective on the historical moments we've explored in this book. Whether it's a holiday greeting or a simple hello to a loved one, these cards are your way to connect with the history we've uncovered together.

Happy creating!

Activity answers

Chapter 1

1.b) Hawaii

2. b) Dalai Lama

3. d) Antarctic Treaty

4. c) St. Lawrence Seaway

5. d) Nikita Khrushchev

6. a) Charles de Gaulle

7. c) Jawaharlal Nehru

8. b) Dwight D. Eisenhower

Chapter 2

1. Mack the Knife

2. The Battle of New Orleans

3. Lonely Boy

4. Venus

Chapter 3

2. Pop Art

3. The Haunting of Hill House

4. A Separate Peace

5. Archibald Prize

6. Avant-garde movements

7. The Tin Drum

Keyword: Flowers for Algernon

Chapter 4:

1. a) Alex Olmedo

2. b) Montreal Canadiens

3. b) Los Angeles Dodgers

4. d) Nicola Pietrangeli

5. a) Baltimore Colts

6. b) Oxo

7. a) Canada

8. b) Brazil

Chapter 6:

1. The USSR's Luna 2 and Luna 3

   The US satellite Explorer 6

2. Boeing 707 Jet Airliner

3. Xerox 914

4. M1 Motorway

5. De Beers manufactures a synthetic Diamond

Chapter 8:

1. a) Jason Alexander

2. b) d) Mike Pence

3. a) Jason Alexander

4. b) Fred Couples

5. c) Simon Cowell

6. d) Allison Janney

7. d) Sean Bean

Embracing 1959: A Grateful Farewell

Step Into 1959: A Celebration of Enduring Stories

Be a part of our tribute to the indomitable spirit of 1959, a year that brimmed with tales of triumph and advancement. Let's embark on a journey through its defining moments, unraveling the threads that have woven its timeless impact on our world.

Preserving Memories, Sharing History's Path.

Your presence has illuminated the chapters of 1959 with your unique perspectives. Your contributions hold immense value in upholding the essence of this groundbreaking year. Together, let's embrace the legacy of '59 and safeguard its significance for generations to cherish.

Thank you for joining us on this unforgettable voyage.
Let the spirit of '59 continue to inspire and resonate with us all.

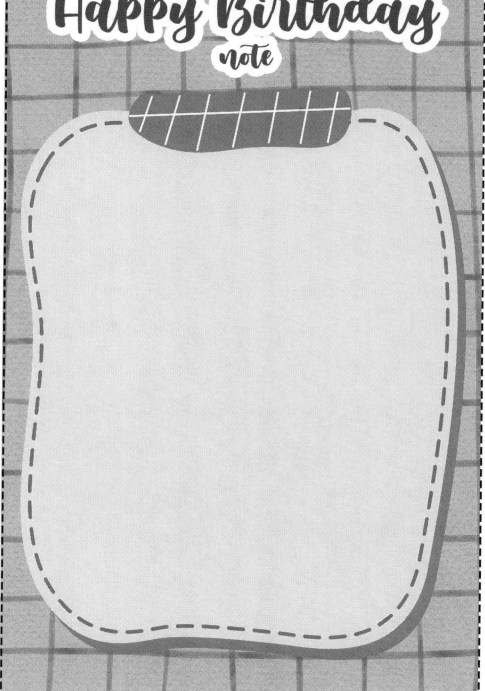

Happy Birthday
note

Happy Birthday
note

HAPPY BIRTHDAY NOTE

TO DO LIST

Name: _____ Day: _____ Month: _____

No	To Do List	Yes	No

TO DO LIST

Name: _____   Day: _____   Month: _____

No	To Do List	Yes	No

TO DO LIST

Name: _____ Day: _____ Month: _____

No	To Do List	Yes	No

NOTE

NOTE

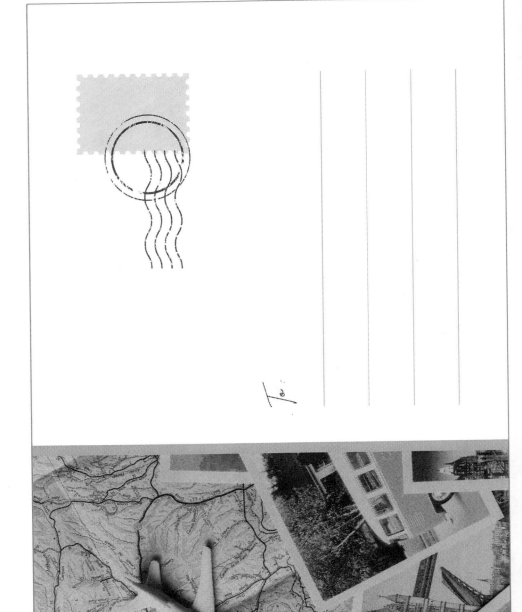

Remember This!
Mill Pond
Winnisimet
Pulling Point
ISLAND
Dorchester Point
SPECTACLE ISLAND

WISH YOU WERE HERE,
123 ANYWHERE ST., ANY CITY

POSTCARD

To:

_____

From: